For my family, my ancestors, my country DmG

For Nevayah, my strong little Dagoman & Arrernte girl SC

This story includes Tasmanian Aboriginal words.
The palawa language words are written in lower case.
See the last page for a glossary of the words used in this book.

luwa tara
luwa waypa

three kangaroos
three Tasmanian Aboriginal men

Dave mangenner Gough

Illustrated by
Samantha Campbell

ABORIGINAL
STUDIES PRESS

In the village, niyakara tells his family he is going to hunt tara, kangaroo.

He collects his spears, waddy and throwing stick.

On his mind is the chief's daughter, tuminana. He knows that she, his sister and some of the village girls and women are at the water, collecting shells and working.

He likes tuminana and just wants to see her before he goes further away from the village to hunt.

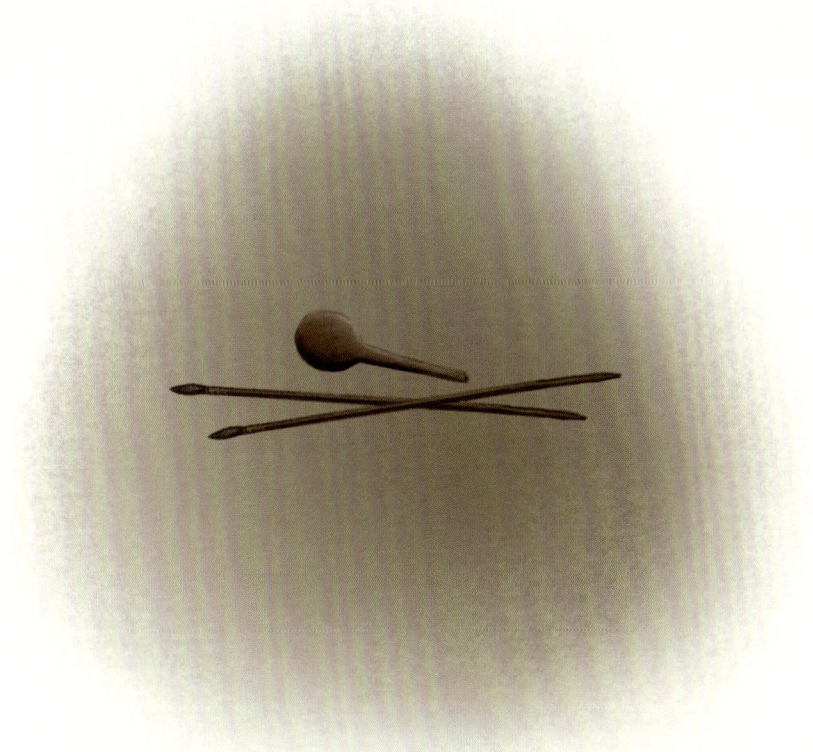

niyakara doesn't want tuminana to know how he feels, as he isn't sure what the chief and his family will think, or even how she feels about him. He thinks she may like him too, but he is very nervous about doing the wrong thing or being laughed at by everyone.

He quietly approaches the beach where the women are and he can see them working, talking and laughing together.

He sits where they can't see him and he watches them for a moment, knowing he shouldn't really be there as this is women's time.

Then, to his surprise, he hears three thuds on the ground nearby.

boom   boom   boom

He looks around to where the sounds seem to come from and sees three warriors hiding, three men he has never seen before.

niyakara's heart starts to beat in his chest.

boom boom   boom boom   boom boom

He lies down and watches the men watching the women.

He wonders, who are they? Where did they come from?

The three warriors get down low to the ground so the women can't see them.

niyakara can see they are pointing and talking about the women.

boom boom   **boom boom**   **boom boom**

The men split up in different directions, signalling to each other as they creep along.

niyakara is looking and can see tuminana and his sisters have no idea they are being watched.

boom boom   **boom boom**   **boom boom**

niyakara's mind is racing. What will happen if they take the girls away, his sisters and tuminana?

What are they going to do? What if they round them up and capture the girls? What if they take them away, his sisters and tuminana?

What should he do? If he makes a noise the warriors could hurt the girls. If he doesn't do anything, they will be ambushed.

The young warrior calls out to moinee.

moinee   moinee   moinee

'Show me what to do, moinee. Help me, moinee.'

He can hardly breathe, his heart is pounding and he feels weak with fear.

boom boom   boom boom   boom boom

niyakara knows that if he leaves to get help, the warriors may ambush him and the girls will be taken.

He can't leave the girls. He keeps watching.

He knows on his own he cannot defend the girls against these three warriors.

He asks moinee again to help him protect the girls. He calls to moinee, his creation spirit.

moinee   moinee   moinee

'Give me the strength and courage of three warriors.'

niyakara puts all his faith in moinee and starts to creep along towards the girls, his heart thumping.

boom boom   boom boom   boom boom

But he feels different. He feels stronger and feels he can, and has to, defend and protect them.

He sees the warriors getting closer to the girls and he panics. Again niyakara calls out.

moinee   moinee   moinee

He sees the warriors starting to signal to each other as they begin to make their move.

niyakara sees an ochre-stained stone right next to his hand, a sign from moinee. He picks it up.

The warriors have seen him.

niyakara sings out with all his heart:

moinee   moinee   moinee

His voice echoes and sounds like three warriors singing out to creation.

He throws the stone towards the warrior closest to the girls and POW! it hits him in the head and ricochets, hitting the second warrior in the back. niyakara turns and then runs towards the third warrior and throws his throwing stick, yelling and screaming.

'Go away.'

The girls all look up and see the strange warriors, and they scream out for help.

boom boom   boom boom   boom boom

The warriors yell to each other and run away down the beach. niyakara runs after them.

His chest pumps up as he runs past the girls. He can see the chief's daughter, tuminana, and his sisters and they all yell out.

'Go, niyakara.'

niyakara yells at the warriors again.

'Go, go, go.'

niyakara chases them further and further and, as he gets close to the end of the beach where the tea-tree starts, he sees something he cannot believe.

In full running strides the warriors seem to be launching away further with every step, almost bouncing, not running. With every step they get further away and with every bounce become more like kangaroos than men.

They cut from side to side, bouncing fast and strong. They are kangaroos, large foresters, in full flight.

niyakara stops and watches them bound away. He can't believe what he has just seen, his heart still thumping in his chest from the biggest chase of his life.

niyakara sits down and rubs his eyes. Then he starts the long walk back.

But as he gets closer to where the girls had been, he can't see them. They are gone. His heart thumps again.

boom boom   **boom boom**   **boom boom**

Where are they? Are they okay? Was he tricked by the warriors? Did they come back and take the girls?

niyakara starts to run back to the village. He feels sick as he runs.

What if they have been taken? What will he say to everyone?

As he approaches the village he hears yelling and singing.

niyakara is back!

niyakara is back!

niyakara is back!

niyakara walks into the village and sees his sister. He sees all the women, and he sees tuminana.

He is greeted by everyone singing his praise.

niyakara warrior!   **boom boom boom**

niyakara warrior!   **boom boom boom**

niyakara warrior!   **boom boom boom**

They pick him up and carry him to a special place by the big fire, next to the chief and two other male elders.

Everyone in the village dances and sings around the fire.

niyakara warrior!   **niyakara warrior!**   **niyakara warrior!**

moinee   **moinee**   **moinee**

niyakara warrior!   **niyakara warrior!**   **niyakara warrior!**

boom boom   **boom boom**   **boom boom**

niyakara thanks moinee for looking after him, tuminana and the girls.

moinee, thank you   **moinee, thank you**   **moinee, thank you**

Later in the evening, niyakara, the chief and the two other elders are the only ones left by the fire.

There is silence.

The chief asks niyakara, 'What happened, young man?'

niyakara swallows a lump in his throat. His heart races again.

He thinks, what do I say? Will they think I am making up stories? Will they think I am crazy?

niyakara can't look at the elders.

'There were three warriors spying on the girls,' he says. 'I chased them away.'

'Is that all that happened?' asks the chief.

'Yes,' says niyakara.

niyakara keeps looking into the fire.
He can't look at the elders as he feels they will know he is not telling them everything.
There is a long silence.

Finally, niyakara raises his head and turns to look at his elders.

To his shock and amazement the elders are not men any more.

They are three large forester kangaroo bucks. They jump up and start bouncing around the fire, flicking their tails and kicking up the sand and sparks. Then they bounce off with large bounds and are gone, as quick as that.

niyakara sits there for a minute, his head spinning, and rubs his eyes.
He feels exhausted and decides to just lie down next to the fire for a while.
He falls asleep for a bit. Three large cracks from the fire wake him up.

crack   crack   crack

He sits up quickly and looks at the fire.

There, he sees the faces of his three elders in the fire, smiling at him.
Then they gradually fade away.

From that day onwards, when niyakara goes off into the bush, he runs as fast as he can, ducking and weaving through the scrub and trees, bouncing from rock to rock. Bouncing further and further each time.

He cuts through the wind and dodges the bush with precision and ease, as he knows how.

He also is tara.

He is also the kangaroo.

tara   tara   tara

ABOUT THE AUTHOR

Dave mangenner Gough is a celebrated artist, curator and cultural practitioner dedicated to practising and demonstrating Tasmanian Aboriginal culture for all Australian people, to bring communities together and preserve our traditional culture.

As a proud trawlwoolway man – descended from Bungana (chief) manalargenna's oldest daughter woretemoeteyemer of north-east Tasmania – Dave has a strong personal connection to lutruwita Tasmania and its people.

As an artist, he has exhibited nationally and internationally. He has also curated a number of significant exhibitions. With Dave as writer, director, producer and performer, *luwa tara luwa waypa* has been performed in Tasmania as part of *mapali dawn gathering*, launching the 2021 Ten Days on The Island arts festival.

ABOUT THE ILLUSTRATOR

Samantha Campbell grew up in the Northern Territory and lives in Alice Springs. She is descended from the Dagoman people from Katherine and as a child lived in remote communities across the Top End. Her first book, *Alfred's War*, written by Rachel Bin Salleh, was shortlisted for the New South Wales Premier's Literary Awards and the Speech Pathology Australia's Book of the Year Awards. Her other books include *Aunty's Wedding* by Miranda Tapsell and Joshua Tyler, *Brother Moon* by Maree McCarthy Yoelu, and *Freedom Day* by Rosie Smiler and Thomas Mayor.

GLOSSARY OF TASMANIAN ABORIGINAL (PALAWA) WORDS

luwa (lu wah) – three

moinee – muyini (moy yee nee) – creator of palawa, the first black man, the rivers and the ground

niyakara (nee yah kah rah) – (to) dream

palawa (pah lah wah) – Tasmanian Aboriginal person

tara (tah rah) – kangaroo (male)

tuminana (tu mee nah nah) – little (fairy) penguin

waddy (wad dee) – a club or stick

waypa (why pah) – Tasmanian Aboriginal man

To hear the author read this story, scan the QR code below.

First published in 2022
by Aboriginal Studies Press

Copyright © Text Dave mangenner Gough 2022
Copyright © Illustrations Samantha Campbell 2022

All rights reserved. No part of this book may be reproduced or transmitted in any form or by any means, electronic or mechanical, including photocopying, recording or by any information storage and retrieval system, without prior permission in writing from the publisher. The Australian *Copyright Act 1968* (the Act) allows a maximum of one chapter or 10 per cent of this book, whichever is the greater, to be photocopied by any educational institution for its education purposes provided that the educational institution (or body that administers it) has given a remuneration notice to Copyright Agency (Australia) under the Act.

The opinions expressed in this book are the author's own and do not necessarily reflect the view of AIATSIS or ASP.

Aboriginal Studies Press is the publishing arm of the Australian Institute of Aboriginal and Torres Strait Islander Studies.

GPO Box 553, Canberra, ACT 2601
Phone: (61 2) 6246 1183
Fax: (61 2) 6261 4288
Email: asp@aiatsis.gov.au
Web: www.aiatsis.gov.au/asp/about.html

 A catalogue record for this book is available from the National Library of Australia

(HB) 978-1-922752-06-2
(ePDF) 978-1-922752-07-9

Illustration technique: Hand drawn in Procreate software on iPad Pro using Apple Pencil.

Cover and text design: Joanna Hunt
Author photograph courtesy of the National Gallery of Australia
Illustrator photograph by Gabrielle Fry
Publishing project management: Erica Wagner

Printed by C&C Offset in China in February 2022

10 9 8 7 6 5 4 3 2 1